COUSINS 4

Four Little Girls – One Big World

Yosemite Vacation

Created By Glen McClure   Illustrated By Alice Wang   Written By Uncle Tony

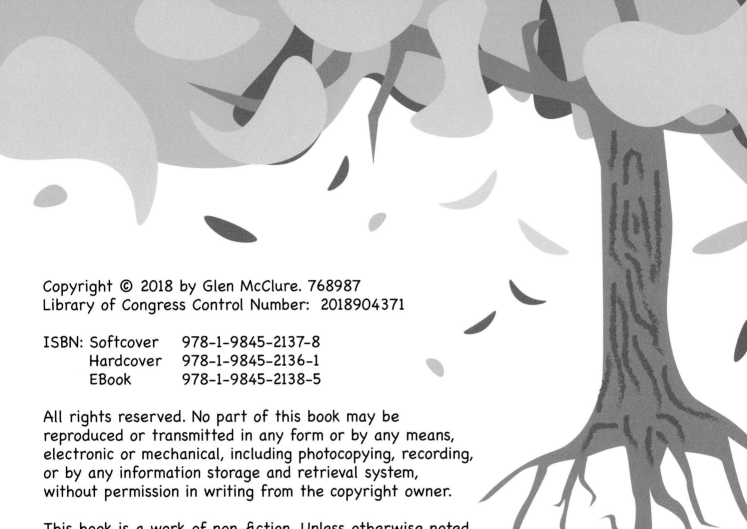

To order additional copies of this book
contact:
Xlibris
1-888-795-4274
www.Xlibris.com
Orders@Xlibris.com

Cousins4 creative team and translators:

With sincere appreciation and recognition of their talent and commitment we proudly acknowledge our Cousins4 creative team.

Created by: Glen McClure
Illustrations and Art Design: Alice Wang
Written by: "Uncle Tony"

Translations:

With gratitude for their professionalism and precision we recognize ou dedicated translating team that clearly and concisely brings Cousins4 a global family of readers:

Chinese: Shuai Wang
Japanese: Keiko Kumamoto
Spanish: Danny Garcia

Dear Parents – Guardians – Caretakers:

Cousins4 chronicles the experiences, relationships and antics of two sets of sisters, who though related as cousins are separated by country and culture. Novva, the eldest at six years of age and Vinne who is four, live in Shanghai with their father a commercial air line pilot and their mom a yoga practioner and instructor. The family often travels internationally providing the sisters with unique insights into different cultures and customs. Their cousins, Kiki who is five and sibling Tami who is three, reside in San Francisco. Their dad, a successful technology entrepreneur and their mother a talented and respected artist, likewise believe that global travel insures a greater appreciation for different countries and respect for their traditions.

The illustrations and writing herein depict the discovery, joy and perceptions, of the four cousins, as they travel, experience, learn and grow. Each cousin is proudly multi-lingual and familiar with various cultures. Every Cousins4 edition will portray an actual event perhaps embellished to provide a more child centric, whimsical and entertaining adventure. We now invite you to share, with your children, this fun and heartwarming edition of Cousins4 and acquaint your family with our family while living, learning and growing with Novva, Kiki, Vinne and Tami. COUSINS4

Park Entrance

"**Yay!** We're almost in **Yosemite**. Look at all the trees and mountains" says Novva. Will we see animals soon? The park ranger says "Yes, you'll see them when you go hiking. They're everywhere. But don't bother them".

"Yeh!优诗美地国家公园说，Novva。我们会很快见到动物吗？公园管理员说："但是不要打扰他们。我不会，她说。

「はい！ヨセミテNovvaは言います。我々は、すぐに動物を見るのでしょうか？パークレンジャー」と言うが、彼らを気にしないでください。私は彼女の言うことはありません。

Yeh!Yosemite dice Novva. Vamos a ver los animales pronto? El Park Ranger dice "pero no les molesta.No lo dice.

Tunnel

"Oh a tunnel!" **cries** Vinne.

"A dark, scary tunnel."

"Don't be afraid" says Kiki.
The park ranger says, "When we go through it, we'll see deer, squirrels and eagles."

"欧！一条隧道！"Vinne大喊，"一条又黑又可怕的隧道！"
"不要害怕。"Kiki说。
护林员告诉她们："当我们穿过隧道，我们就会看见小鹿，松鼠还有老鹰。"

「あっトンネル！」とヴィニが泣きそうになりながらいいます。「まっくらでこわーいトンネルだよ。」
「だいじょうぶ、こわくないよ。」キキがいうと、パークレンジャーは、「トンネルをとおったら、きっとシカやリス、ワシにもあえるよ。」

"¡Hurra! Estamos casi en Yosemite. Mira todos los árboles y montañas ", dice Novva.
Novva. "¿Vamos a ver animales pronto?"
El guardabosque dice: "Sí, los verás cuando vayas de excursión". Están por todas partes pero
no los molestes ".
"No lo haré", dice ella.

Campsite

Kiki says "Our **campsite** is set up. "Let's go swimming".
Nova "No let's go hiking."
Vinne "No let's climb trees."
Tami "I'm hungry, let's eat."

Kiki说 "我们的营地搭建好啦，去游泳吧！"
Novva说 "不，我们去徒步探险！"
Vinne说 "不，我们去爬树！"
Tami说 "我饿了，我们去吃东西吧。"

「テントもたてたし、およぎにいこうよ。」とキキがいいました。
「ちがうよ、ハイキングにいこう。」とノバ、
「いやだいやだ、木のぼりしようよ。」とヴィニ、
「おなかすいたぁ、おひるにしようよ。」とたみがいいます。

Kiki dice "Nuestro campamento está completo. Vamos a nadar."
Nova "No, vamos a escalar las montañas ".
Vinne "No, trepemos los árboles".
Tami "Tengo hambre, comamos".

Campfire

Kiki: " Today I swam in a river."
Novva: "Hiking was fun."
Vinne: "I climbed a pine tree."
Tami: "Lunch was good. Is it dinner time yet?"

Kiki "今天我去小河里游泳了。"
Novva "徒步探险太有趣了！"
Vinne "今天我爬上了一棵松树。"
Tami "午餐很好吃，晚餐时间到了吗？"

「きょうはかわでおよいだよ。」とキキがいうと、
「ハイキングはたのしかったぁ。」とノバ、
「パインの木にのぼったの。」とヴィニ、
「おひるごはんおいしかったぁ、ところでよるごはんはまだか
なぁ?とタミはいいました。

Kiki "Hoy nadé en un río".
Novva "Escalar las montañas fue divertido".
Vinne "Trepé a un árbol de pino".
Tami "El almuerzo estuvo delicioso. ¿Ya es hora de
cenar?

The Shuttle

Novva "I hope the shuttle takes us to a meadow with animals and birds."

Kiki "I want to see a **waterfall**."

Vinne "We better be going high up in the **mountains.**"
Tami "Can we drive to the village for a snack?"

Novva "我希望摆渡车会带我们去一片有很多鸟儿和动物的草地。"
Kiki "我想去看瀑布。"
Vinne "我们最好去山的最高处。"
Tami "我们可以开去小村子找点零食吗？"

「バスがどうぶつやとりたちがいるところにつれていってくれないかなぁ。」ノバはおもいます。
「たきがみたいなぁ。」とキキ。
「たかいたかいやまのうえにいくのがとうぜんよね。」とヴィニ。
「バスでおやつかいにヴィレッジにいきたいな…」とタミ。

Novva "Espero que el transporte nos lleve a un prado con animales y pájaros".
Kiki "Quiero ver las cataratas".
Vinne "Será mejor que vayamos a lo alto de las montañas".
Tami "¿Podemos ir al pueblo a comer algo?"

Water Fall

Standing a safe distance from Yosemite Falls, Novva looks up and says. "Look an **EAGLE**".
Kiki enjoys the mist from the falls. An excited Vinne says

"Cousins **look** at all the fish!" and Tami stands back and finishes her ice cream cone.

站在优胜美地瀑布前，Novva 抬头看便喊起来:"快看！一只老鹰！"
Kiki享受着瀑布吹起的水雾。兴奋的Vinne 喊到:"姐姐妹妹们，快看，好多鱼！"
Tami站在后面美美地吃完了一个冰激凌甜筒。

ヨセミテのたきのちかくにきましたノンバはタイをしたからみあげいみんなり，めげうは
キーはきのみずしぶきをへびってたのしんでいます。ワイニも
まうちむなから「みてみのかりをかみだより」
タミはらいかいわらずしろでアイスクリームをべロベロしています

De pie a una distancia segura de las cataratas de Yosemite, Novva mira hacia arriba y dice: "Mira, un águila".
Kiki disfruta de la niebla de las cataratas. Vinne muy emocionada dice: "primas, miren a todos los peces", y
Tami se detiene y termina un cono de helado.

Hiking Day

Kiki wants the cousins to follow her and leads the way.

"Hiking is **fun**," says Novva. "We'll walk and talk and stay on the trail."

Kiki领着表姐妹们跟着她走。
"徒步太好玩了，"Novva 说，"我们边走边说一路向前。"

キキはイトコたちぜんいんをみちびこうとがんばります。
「あーたのしい！」とノバはごきげん。「みんなであるいてしゃべってコースをいくの。」

Kiki quiere que los primas la sigan y guíe el camino. "El senderismo es divertido", dice Novva. "Caminaremos, hablaremos y nos mantendremos en el camino".

Deer Sighting

"Look! Cousins a baby deer." says Vinne.
"A baby deer is called a fawn." says Novva.
Kiki explains, "A papa deer is called buck."
Tami adds "And a mama deer is a doe."

"看啊，姐妹们，一只小鹿，"Vinne叫到。
"小鹿就是fawn，"Novva说。
Kiki说，"小鹿的爸爸就是Buck。"
Tami补充道，"鹿妈妈叫Doe。"

「あっみんな、シカのあかちゃんよ」とヴィニ
がいいました。
「しかって、ってよぶんだよ。」とノバがよく言
はいいます。
けどうさんシカはおしかっていうのよ」と
タミもいいません。

"Miren, primos, un venado bebé", dice Vinne.
"Un venado bebé se llama un cervatillo",
dice Novva.
Kiki dice "Un venado papa se llama ciervo".
Tami dice "Y un venado mama se llama
cierva."

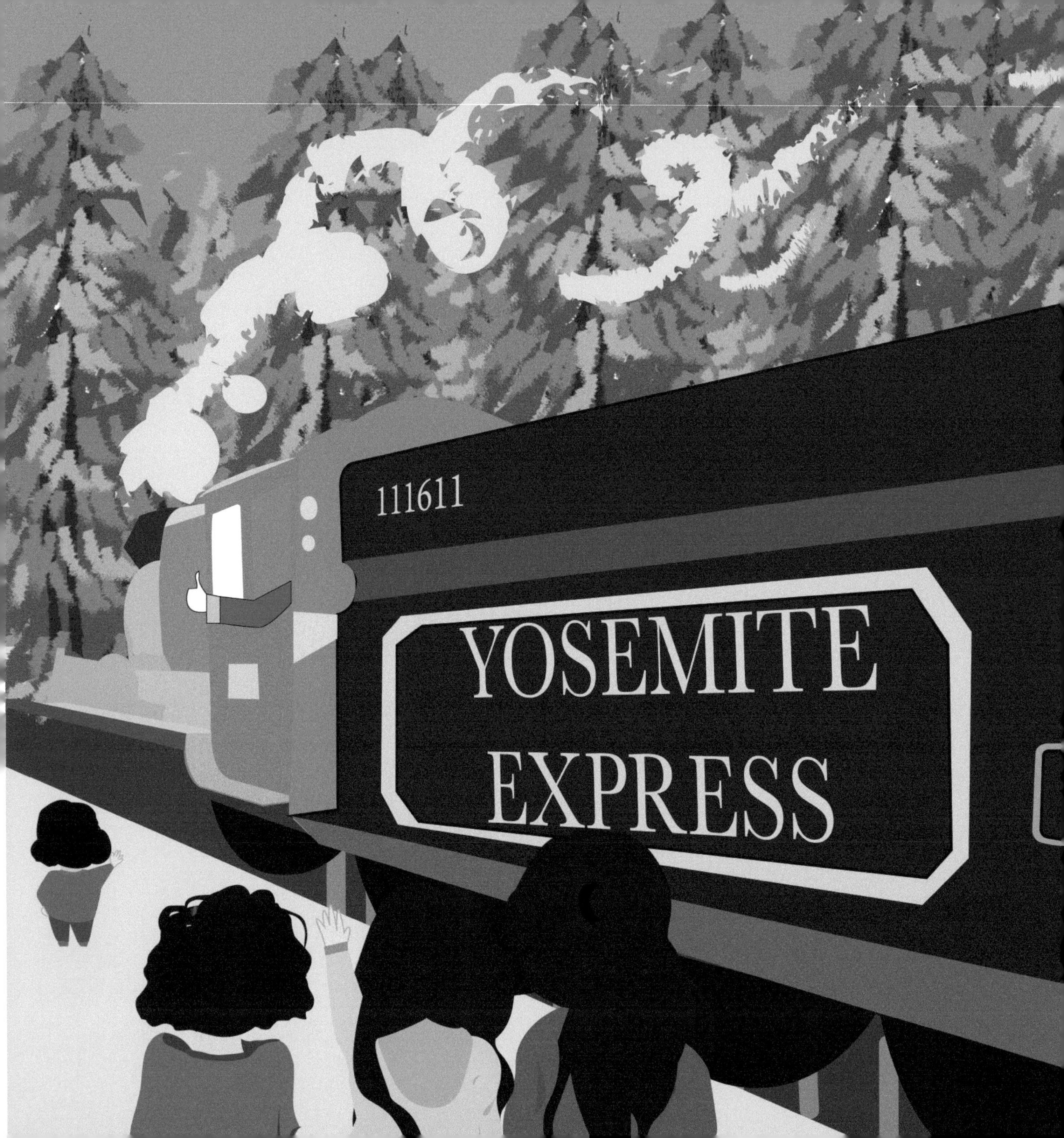
111611
YOSEMITE
EXPRESS

Sugar Pine Railroad

While riding the Yosemite steam train, the cousins enjoy the scenery. Engineer Joe says. "This train is over a hundred years old and is driven daily by ME."

Novva hopes they'll see Yosemite Falls, and Vinne is looking for Half Dome. "We'll stop at both places" says Joe.

Kiki loves the old train and Tami says. "My train in San Francisco is nicer."

坐在优胜美的地的蒸汽火车上，表姐妹们享受着沿路的美景。列车长Joe说："

这火车已经一百多岁了，我每天都开着它。"

Novva希望能在火车上看见瀑布，Vinne在找着半圆顶山。

"我们会在这两个地方靠站的。"Joe说道。

Kiki很喜欢老火车，Tami说:"我在旧金山家里的火车比这个更漂亮。"

イトコたちはヨセミテれっしゃにのって、かわっていくそとのけしきをたのしんでいます。そこにしゃしょうさんのジョーがきて、

このきしゃは100ねんもうごいていて、まいにちわたしがうんてんしているんだよ。」といいました。

ノバはヨセミテのたきを、ヴィニはハーフドームをみたがっているみたいです。

ジョーは「どちらにもとまるからね。」とふたりをあんしんさせます。

E-キキはとてもきしゃがきにいったよう。タミは「サンフランシスコのでんしゃのほうがかっこういいよ。」とつぶやきます。

Mientras viajan en el tren a vapor de Yosemite, los primos disfrutan del paisaje. El director Joe dice:

"Este tren tiene más de cien años y yo lo manejo todos los días".

Novva espera ver Yosemite Falls, y Vinne está buscando Half Dome.

"Nos detendremos en ambos lugares", dice Joe.

Kiki le encanta el viejo tren, y Tami dice: "Mi tren en San Francisco es más agradable".

Bye Bye Yosemite

As the cousins exit Yosemite, each is excited to share their experience.

Novva said, "I learned a lot about plants and animals." Kiki shouted!,

"I can't wait to tell my classmates about Yosemite." Vinne comment-
ed, "When I grow up. I want to be a park ranger."
Tami asked, "Are we home yet?"

离开优胜美地的时候，表姐妹们互相分享着各自的经历。
Novva说:"我认识了很多植物和动物。"
Kiki惊叹道:"我都等不及去告诉我的同学们了。"
Vinne说:"等我长大以后要做个护林员。"
Tami问道:"我们到家了么？"

ヨセミテをでたあと、イトコたちはおたがいけいけんしたことを、はなしあうことにしました。
「わたしはしょくぶつやどうぶつのことをたくさんならったわ。」とノバ。
「はやくヨセミテのことをクラスメートにおはなししたいなぁ。」とおおごえでいいます。
「わたしはおおきくなったらパークレンジャーになるわ！」とヴィニははりきっています。
E-「おうちまだぁ〜？」とタミはきくばかり。

A medida que las primas salen de Yosemite, cada una está emocionada de
compartir su experiencia.
Novva dijo: "Aprendí mucho sobre plantas y animales".
Kiki exclamó: "¡No puedo esperar para contarle a mis compañeras sobre
Yosemite!"
Vinne comentó: "Cuando sea grande, quiero ser una guardabosque".
E-Tami preguntó: "¿Ya llegamos a casa?

Rhyme Time
Yosemite Vacation

Novva says: "Kiki, Vinne, Tami, and Me
went hiking and biking in Yosemite.
We saw mountains and rivers and trees
everywhere.
And early one morning a deer and a bear.
At our campsite at night we cooked on a fire
told stories and laughed and sang like a choir.
But soon we'll go home with a sweet memory
About hiking and biking in Yosemite."

Glen McClure

Reflecting upon my childhood in suburban Los Angeles and subsequent achievements leading to a variety of management positions in China, my personal journey was methodical yet upwardly mobile. As a child I was inspired by a solid family dynamic and the positive influences of a tight knit multi-cultural community. I was fortunate to be mentored by caring parents and dedicated teachers. This special synergy that combines a strong family structure with abundant educational opportunities encouraged my participation in various childhood pursuits. Numerous team and group activities like Baseball, Scouting and swimming taught me the importance of preparation, teamwork and just having fun. My skill as a tradesman underscores the training and mentoring provided by my father, a successful building contractor. Working summer jobs with him and following his example was inspiring because he demonstrated the importance of a strong work ethic and completing projects in a timely and professional manner. I would be remiss if I failed to recognize my mother, sister and two brothers who each in their own special way was a positive influence for which I am most grateful.

My career began humbly as a factory worker then blossomed into numerous management positions within the same multi- national conglomerate. Subsequent to my forty years with this company I founded McClure Global, a diversified Los Angeles and Shanghai based manufacturing and consulting firm. As CEO I continue to travel frequently. My total of thirty countries and 4 continents visited includes travel to China, South Korea, Peru, India, Mexico and Romania. Indeed the customs and culture of each of these nations has positively impacted my personal world view and made me not just a better business person but no doubt a better person. As I approach retirement I now have the flexibility to delegate most business functions and enjoy the benefits of being a doting grandfather. This special time, in my life, inspires my willingness to document the the collective and individual experiences of my four darling granddaughters with the publication of Cousins4 - Edition #1. Well enough about me. Say hello to these four smart, cute and curious little angels and share with your family the beautifully illustrated and heartwarming travels and experiences of Novva, Kiki, Vinne and Tami. COUSINS4.

Printed in the United States
By Bookmasters